BELICHICK: Your Best Movie Villain in Sports

William Russo

LONG TIME AGO BOOKS

Imprint: Independently published

ISBN: 9798594952898

Introduction

If you read the breadth of humorous pieces done on Bill Belichick over the past decade with the same eye as I have used to write them, you will note that two features dominate the blogs.

First, he is often the co-star to Tom Brady. He usually takes the role of nemesis or friendly enemy. He is never second banana. But, his role in the Patriot entries and comical asides almost always depicts him as secondary to Tom.

Another feature about Coach Belichick jumped out at me as I collected some of the blog entries: he is often associated with movie counterparts. And, this comparison is hardly flattering. Belichick invariably comes across as a James Bond-style villain. That's not to say he is less important, but he may be the most important figure in Patriots lore.

What's more he is adaptable to many kinds of movie archetypes. So, as you read these pieces, you may find reference to great movies and great characters to which he dovetails rather neatly.

Belichick could be Boris Badenov or Wile E. Coyote.

Movie Mashed Up

In a move of brilliant desperation, Coach Bill Belichick decided to take his beleaguered New England Patriots to see a holiday movie at a penultimate moment of the season.

No, they are not watching *Elf, Miracle on 34th Street,* nor *A Christmas Carol* (which might offer insights into the psychology of their mercurial coach).

Instead, Belichick took his team's mind off mayhem and NFL assassination attempts by showing them life on the other side: *Lone Survivor* is about a Navy Seals mission in Afghanistan in 2007.

It was a movie to provide a 21st century rallying cry that rivals "Remember the Alamo" or "Remember Pearl Harbor".

Wags thought he might take them to the ubiquitous *Anchorman 2* with Ron Burgundy. There was no Chablis or Zinfandel for these players, let alone Burgundy.

Belichick knows what he does. He is preparing a decimated team for warfare. He is not trying to take their minds of battle, but make them aware of what defines sacrifice and valor.

Mark Wahlberg is a local New Englander who stars and produces the film—and may have hinted to Belichick that this was the pick of the season. It will certainly give Wahlberg's box office a shot.

A private screening for over 50 Patriots and supporting staff likely did the trick in both resting the physical bodies of debilitated NFL warriors and recharging the spirit of American heroism.

Movies used to do that for all its citizens, whether it was *The Sands of Iwo Jima* or *The Fighting Sullivans.*

Now it is left to the young men who represent the best of America's economic and social heroism: our football players. The last real Patriots took in a movie about the last real patriots.

New England Coaching

Brad Stevens photo morphed 20 years into future.

Coach of the Boston Celtics Brad Stevens could not ignore the two-ton elephant in the Celtics locker room.

Everyone thought that Rajon Rondo, injured and rehabbing his knee, would simply dominate the new callow coach.

But not a month into the season, Rondo has not had to put on his dominatrix outfit once. Brad Stevens has proven to be simply simpatico to his mercurial point guard.

Stevens is the perfect match for temperamental point guards and frustrated court generals. Rondo and Stevens each like three-dimensional chess and will not let Boston basketball deteriorate into Hooverville hoops.

Instead of eating Coach Stevens alive, as some feared, Rondo looks like the cat that swallowed the canary. He sits on the bench nightly and admires his new coach. It is a far cry from the days of daily battles with Doc Rivers.

Instead, Rondo has put a photograph of New England Patriots coach Bill Belichick on the wall in Brad's office. Rondo used to make trips to Foxboro like a kid standing at the window of the toy store, wishing he had one of those.

And, Stevens seems to be taking the role model to heart. When nutcase Marcus Smart threw up the buzz-beater winning 3-point shot against the Heat, Brad had no visible reaction to winning the game.

This sort of behavior makes the stoical Rondo look like the man who broke the bank at Monte Carlo. When Coach Stevens speaks about *sang-froid,* it drives Rondo mad with passion.

Rondo has already picked out a Christmas present for Coach Stevens: it's a gray hoodie with cutoff sleeves. The fit is just about right.

Pat Patriot & British Umpire

The Patriots will face their toughest opponent on Sunday night. And, no, it is not the Indianapolis Colts. It's not even the benighted and bewitching referees that hold the fate of bettors everywhere in their hands. It's not the point spread, and it's not some sports intangible.

The Patriots in the fourth quarter will go up against the formidable *Downton Abbey*. It will be Foxboro Abbey versus Downton on the lush green cricket field.

PBS does not blink for CBS.

Lord and Lady Grantham, also known as the Earl and Countess, have too much class to talk openly about beating up the ratings neighbors, but the Patriots are Americans. Fans will tell you Lady Grantham is American and likely will root for them secretly.

We are here to tell you that his Lordship just did battle with the family and staff about having one of those blasted "wireless" contraptions brought into Downton. Only the King's speech could convince him to stand for it.

We have serious doubt he will let a large screen TV and a potential Super Bowl party into the main drawing room. He relegated the wireless to the "small library."

Rose and Lady Edith are innovators and might be fans of Tom Brady (both desperate for a good leader to save them from Lady Mary who is fickle and seems to find good men as quick as she discards them).

The most likely fans of Gronk at Downton are Tom, the former chauffeur, and Thomas Barrow, the gay underbutler. As for the rest of downstairs staff, we expect they will stay loyal to the Dowager Countess who remains Bill Belichick's biggest supporter. Not a trick gets past her.

Onto the Yellow Brick Road

The Wiz

Unlike T-Rex Ryan of Jurassic Buffalo, Chipmunk Kelly wants to kill the Patriots with kindness. How else do you explain the syrupy mess that he has oozed all over Bill Belichick and Tom Brady?

T-Rex won't genuflect and kiss the rings of Belichick, but Chipper the K is ready to canonize the Patriots and send them to the NFL equivalent of nirvana in Canton, Ohio.

We cannot dispute the politically correct Kelly. Bill Belichick will give him more than the time of day at the end of the game on Sunday when the Patriots will kick the Eagle out of his aerie and take the Emerald City.

Kelly likely hopes his kindness will beget kindness from the master of strategic kill. Belichick has not been able to issue any "take no prisoners" order lately.

Belichick has had a week to think about not having anyone with true ability to catch a Brady pass. There will be compensations made and dispensations not given. We expect his brain-trust aides have found new ways to defend onslaughts on Brady's crown by stopping him from falling down and breaking into pieces.

If the Great Hoodie is anything like Queen Latifah playing the Great Oz, he will use all his guile to keep anyone on the Eagles from discovering that the wizard behind the curtain is a little man using great PR.

This is Belichick's moment to show that the Wizard of Foxboro Park can dispatch any of the evil sisters of the NFL with their flying monkeys in referee suits.

If *The Wiz Live* can be a big hit on TV as its Broadway tryout, then the Patriots may take the cue and not let the House of NFL land on their star quarterback.

Twilight Time

Has the Grinch stolen the Patriots Super Bowl 50?

Roger Goodell is smiling ear-to-ear this week.

For the better part of 17 years, fans of football have thought Bill Belichick was the Grinch, but now he is clearly off the hook. Scrooge, yes. Grinch, no.

We suppose that Cam Newton is wearing his Grinch outfit this year, pretender to the throne. If you want a throwback to Tom Brady a decade ago, Cam Newton is your clone. Send in the clones.

Apparently Tom Brady has used up his three wishes—and now the evil sorcerer Roger Goodell is about to drop a house on the Patriots candidate for the Ponce de Leon Award.

Watching the Patriots lose a second game in a row has been like trying to finish a 2000-piece jigsaw puzzle, only to discover a key piece in dead center is missing.

The genie in the bottle has popped out, if not pooped out, and stolen Tom's magical flying carpet.

Some smart-aleck trolls on the Internet have taken to saying that it's time for the Patriots to start cheating again. On our part we have never considered using the supernatural to win the Super Bowl to be anything but a quantum physics.

However, it's beginning to look like Sergeant Pepper's Band has abandoned the Patriots just as the Magical Mystery Tour is about to commence.

If, as Bill Belichick has often said, December is when the real season begins, the Patriots have reverse engineered another winning season. Belichick's DeLorean has four flat tires and an ejection seat that hits the door on the way out

You begin to wonder if Roger Goodell exposed Tom Brady to the Hope Diamond.

Why is this man laughing?

Bill Belichick canceled practice before Wildcard Weekend.

Whether he is supremely confident of his opponent in next week's game (those dangerous Chiefs), or whether he is so cavalier because loss is written on the injury list, only the game will prove.

Instead of practicing for the next round, the Great Hoodie in all his infinite wisdom chose to shock his players by taking them across the street from the field to Patriot Place.

There, at the Kraft family $$ emporium shopping center, the team closed down the bowling alley and took over a new sport.

Yes, the Pats went bowling to prepare for the next match. It may be the most inspired strategy of all. Belichick knows his wounded players are hobbling physically and mentally. So, he showed them he is not worried when he donned an Alfred E. Neumann mask.

Methods in the madness are not new for Belichick. He drives some sports nuts to the new high ground of cashiered coconuts.

As for us, we have grown accustomed to the franchise's unorthodox approach to big games. Hell, we saw the benighted Houston Texans take a Patriot play—and botch it.

We loved seeing **J.J. Watt** and Vince Wilfork try to score on a goal-line rush. It didn't work, but somewhere at Foxboro we knew the Great Hoodie was smiling.

Texan coach O'Brien might have tried putting Tom Brady behind Vince Wilfork for a touchdown, but he was hampered by the Hoyer the water-boy's ineptitude. If you wanted to see a career go down the poop chute, you were on hand for Brian Hoyer's swan song in the NFL.

Such shenanigans are impossible with the Patriots. The Great Hoodie is not some carbon copy, photocopy, Xerox version of football probability. If he chooses to go irreverent, insouciant, or iconoclastic, he knows this blog will approve.

Belichick's Message!

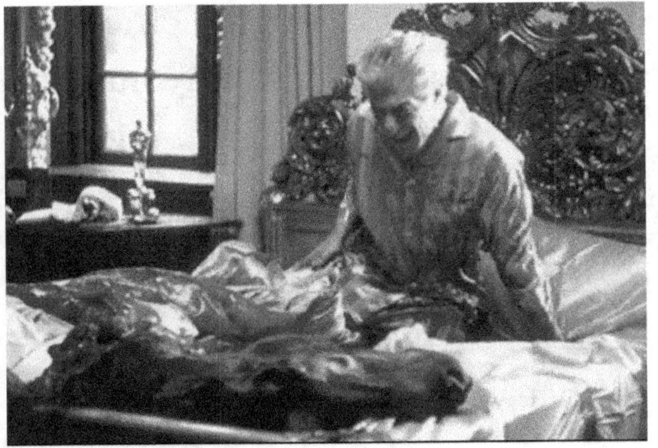

For the third time in three years, the Patriots will find a new doctor to tend to the variety of wobbly knees, bent attitudes, and separated shoulders.

Of course, the present doctor praised the organization and his dream job with the Krafty business. You wouldn't expect a respected professional to be dismissed by Belichick. Dr. Matt Provencher has been associated with Mass. General Hospital. We are not talking about a guesswork meteorologist that irked Bill Belichick.

So, the housecleaning at Patriot Place continues with anyone associated with the weaknesses of this year's team find themselves pushing the revolving door, spinning out quicker and quicker.

You might theorize that rats leave a sinking ship, if you were a Denver Bronco, but you'd be wrong. Belichick is giving a heave-ho and a pushy push-push to anyone who seems askance.

Since these are the staff members who labor for the glory of being with the Patriots, you can imagine what the Great Hoodie has in store for those whose salary towers over their performances.

Bill likes a good return on his dollar—and he likely will find a bunch of unknowns and undrafted John Doe types. They will shine for a season or so under the Hoodie—before wanting big bucks.

As far as we can tell, there are few untouchables in the Belichick caste.

Brady and Gronk seem to be top of the list. Indeed, Patriots will find another Gronkowski brother in the draft, already having interviewed him, to keep Gronk happy. He had another brother on the team a few seasons ago.

As for that notorious O-line that has the same porous quality of the notorious O-ring for NASA thirty years ago, you can expect that Brady's staunch defenders will be unrecognizable come this summer.

Playoff Fever

That notorious Celtics leprechaun has put a pot of gold at the end of the rainbow—and perennial town favorites from the New England football squad are now responding.

Everyone loves a cross-pollinated city of champions.

To that end, New England Patriots owner Robert Kraft and head coach Bill Belichick were courtside fans watching the Celtics win an overtime game against the Atlanta Hawks in the first-round of the NBA Playoffs.

Belichick must enjoy seeing another up and coming genius coach preparing his long career of banners hanging from the TD Garden rafters. Brad Stevens is the successor to the Great Hoodie.

Belichick is no lucky charm, but is a true fan. He also brought his entire coaching staff to game three and planted them all in a luxury box.

IT Boy Isaiah Thomas had high fives and eyes only for recently re-signed bull in a china shop LaGarrette Blount who also sat near the Celtics bench and exchanged support worthy of a mutual admiration society. At game's end on Sunday, IT gave Blount the shirt off his back.

Of course, the majesty of all sports celebrities in Boston nowadays is Gronk who showed up to give his blessing. In fact, he came with one of the other Gronks—not his onesie pals.

Grand Gronk once again managed to outshine Tom Brady (a no-show this time). Tom is likely to come to a game six or seven. He doesn't really throw that magic around until it's needed.

Since winning is contagious, we expect around twelve Patriots to be at the next home game, including the usual suspects like Patrick Chung, Julian Edelman, Danny Amendola, and Matthew Slater who have come to games in past championship runs.

Jabaal the Hutt?

When asked about his defensive players, Coach Swami Belichick became defensive.

Media questions always are offensive at Gillette Stadium, even from the reluctant to make waves local press. But, the press pulled no punches when asking about the "benching" of Jabaar the Hutt Sheard, whose behavior resembles Mr. Christian on the Bounty.

We know who has been set adrift—and Sheard is no Marlon Brando.

And, Belichick is like Charles Laughton: Henry the Eighth and Captain Blight rolled into one. All spelling deliberate. Twenty lashes with a wet noodle for Sheard. His pal Jamie Collins was sent to Siberia, now located in Cleveland, and Sheard wants his own gulag.

To top off the defensive realignment in Foxboro, another defensive star starter will be a non-starter for four weeks. Yep, Alan Branch has been pruned by the NFL for allegedly using marijuana before it is legal in Massachusetts in December.

Someone should have informed him that the liberating vote did not repeal usage immediately.

If you have a sense that the SS Patriot boat has been rocked, you probably have already headed for the lifeboat with Captain Bligh Belichick. We are not witnessing anything akin to *the Caine Mutiny* or *Mutiny on the Bounty*, but we do think Bounty paper towels won't be able to clean up this mess. You Caine count on it.

Will this rock the Patriots, preventing an appearance in the Super Bowl? Or will it send them to the Toilet Bowl without a thought of the post-season, thus ruining Brady's revenge?

Stay tuned, all you defensive stooges. Slowly, Swami Belichick turns...step by step....

Fake Baloney

Fake news has now moved into the sphere of sports in Boston.

A half-baked article has just appeared by some writer named Charlotte Wilder of Lincoln, Massachusetts, (a *hoity-toity* rich town) calling the New England Patriots a team that has a "Trump problem."

It isn't true, but trolls have to spread their venom.

In the old days we'd call this baloney. Today it is simply liberal conspiracy and fake news.

This writer cites one or two people who complain they are completely disillusioned with Tommy Brady and

Bill Belichick. Talk about making a generalization on a small sample size! This sample is practically pea-brained size.

People/Fans claim they will never buy merchandise from the Patriots ever again, and they will not watch a game with their families henceforth.

Most of these quoted isolated cases of Liberals are tickled types who gave dedicated support to Hillary Clinton. However, if you look at real Patriot fans, none of them were really dedicated Clinton supporters; perhaps they are not even dedicated Trump supporters.

The nature of sports is an escape from political fake news and daily life in Massachusetts.

It's entirely possible that the vast majority of Patriot fans still love Brady and begrudgingly admire Belichick. They still regard Belichick as a sports genius and don't even mind Mr. Kraft visiting Trump at Trump Towers.

For most fans politics is a game of hypocrisy.

There's no doubt in far-out Massachusetts many Clinton supporters are now blackballing Trump supporters. We've heard of cases of people refusing to talk to family members who voted for Trump. We know of "friends" who have disparaged their friends who voted for the wrong candidate.

We point out that the people who claim Trump is full of hate are the ones who are showing hate to Trump voters.

When you read about how the Patriots and Brady have alienated Patriot fans, you can relegate this to the fake sports news category.

There is no refuge from political scoundrels.

Over Trump's Wall

All this week the New England Patriots have been in Mexico City, preparing for the big game on Sunday. Coach Bill Belichick is in heaven: he has avoided the New England media all week while in Mexico. For all we know, he may have been in Puerto Viagra, enjoying the sites.

It's possible but coach Bill Belichick is worried about Montezuma's Revenge, which bears a strange resemblance to Roger Goodell's Revenge. At the very least the Oakland Raiders, the opponents of the Trump Patriots, have played in Mexico City last year and may have a very large fan base among those on the wrong side of the Trump Wall.

We look with great expectation to see if the enormous crowd is that greeted Julian Edelman and Danny Amendola this summer in the public relations video movie are indicative of Patriots' support south of the border. Edelman felt like one of the Beatles, but he will not be on the field and has not made the trip.

As far as eating the local cuisine, we know the Patriots bring their own boxed lunches wherever they go. You can never predict when the locals or illegal immigrants will poison the Trump supporters.

We hope none of the players and brush their teeth with tap water. That's only one of the problems when you're 7500 feet up in the air.

We do expect Tom Brady to throw a lot of long balls There's no need for deflation of the ball because it will go further even fully inflated in the super light air.

By flying in their own private jet, we have no worries that ICE troopers and Homeland Security Nazis will be bothering the Patriots. On top of that, you can count on the fact that they have a presidential pardon to escape customs and over those Trump Walls they will fly.

No wonder Jerry Jones is jealous of Robert 'P***y' Kraft.

Boston's Conundrum

Eat your Greens: Hornet & Lantern

For the better part of a decade, there has been no such creature as a head-to-head match-up of the Boston Celtics and the New England Patriots.

It was no contest. We could plead *nolo contendre* with gay abandon.

If the two franchises were playing in the same small timeframe, without question, the attention went directly to Belichick, Brady, and their imitation of 1950s-60s Celtics as a football franchise.

Perhaps in some future date the Patriots will have 17 championships and Bill Belichick and Red Auerbach will march, arm in arm, into New England mythology. Red used to light up a cigar, and Belichick lights up the media. You will see Tom Brady and Bill Russell matching ring for ring on their fingers.

However, this week in Boston, the conundrum rises anew: the Pats are playing on Monday night, and so are the newly rejuvenated Celtics. Normally, Patriots are sitting court-side at the Celtics game—but both teams are on the road and playing simultaneously.

Nineteen-year old shooter Jayson Tatum is leading the league in three-point shooting. We haven't seen a 19-

year old with this kind of dead eye since Billy the Kid shot up the New Mexico league in 1880.

Brady is twice as old as Tatum, but together they could be an epoch of victors lasting half a century. If Jayson Tatum plays until the mid-2040s, he may be retiring at the same age as Tom.

We are not sure whether we will be around for the accolades and retirement ceremony, but it is possible.

Hardly a man is now alive who saw Babe Ruth pitch for the Red Sox, but we are the recipient of modern medical miracles already.

So, whom will you watch on Monday night?

Fortunately, the new age of technology allows us to put the Patriots on our tablet and the Celtics on our smartphone—and leave our other attention to a new movie on UFOs on cable.

Life is grand nowadays. We are riding in the chariots of the gods.

Belichick's Horror Tale

Boris Eliminates Moose

Did Bill Belichick lose his marbles after losing a game?

Have we just witnessed a Pats' version of *Nightmare on Patriot Row*?

Conspiracy theorists have emerged that HC Bill Belichick deliberately sabotaged his own team to lose the Super Bowl. What kind of point was he making in benching his best defensive safety in favor of lesser players?

Did he undermine his own coach Matt Patricia by denying him the player he wanted? Did he punish Patricia for jumping ship to accept another job in Detroit?

Did players in the locker room express anger and disdain for Belichick's unreasonable punishment of Malcolm Butler?

Why have retired players or former players expressed shock at the strategy of the Great Hoodie?

Has the furor and disdain between Tom Brady and Belichick reached the point where Tom can play one of the best games ever as a quarterback and be forced to swallow hard?

Did Belichick make a point to ownership that forced him to trade away his QB of the future, Jimmy G, and keep a 40-year old who has defied his training staff?

Is Bill Belichick forcing the Patriots to make a Hobson's Choice, which centers on whether they should fire the head coach for insubordination?

What kind of media feeding frenzy is possible over this, as facts emerge that there was mutiny in the locker room before game—which showed itself in Malcolm Butler crying on the sidelines?

Egad, is this any way to end a season? To end a year of hard work? What politics has undermined the New England Patriots ultimately from winning a sixth Super Bowl under Belichick and with Tom Brady?

Your Worst Nightmare

The ghost of Malcolm Butler now walks the halls of Patriot Place. Forget the Overlook Hotel and its shining denizens. Foxboro will be a worthy subject for Stephen King.

Like unfriendly spirits, this Patriot specter may hang around for decades, frightening children and bringing back the horrors of Super Bowl LII.

Bad karma often is behind the haunting appearances of ghosts. We recall in Boston that the ghost of Babe Ruth put a curse on the Red Sox for 80 years. We now wonder if the ghost of Malcolm Butler might do the same for the Patriots.

If you wonder why the Patriots never win another Super Bowl in the 21st century, you will be wise to remember that the Butler did it.

Like some benighted head of the Inquisition, Bill Belichick made his decisions to burn the defense at the stake during the Super Bowl. Heretics be damned, and leading the charge was the ingrate (in Swami Belichick's eyes), the man who tried to jump ship before the season began: Malcolm Butler.

It was an unforgivable sin—and now Malcolm Butler has paid for it with his reputation. Oh, someone will give him a big payday—and perhaps he will fade into oblivion in some other football venue.

However, in Foxboro, his curse will be laid upon Tom Brady worse than broken mirrors and contempt for sports superstition.

The howls in the night and the bumps and bangs you hear are the restless spirits of players done dirt by Bill Belichick.

Though he may go into retirement, he will leave a haunted Patriot Place for Josh McDaniels, forcing him to call in ghostbusters and hold séances for the betterment of the Kraft legacy.

Move over, Shirley Jackson, Gillette Stadium is the new house on Haunted Hill.

2-Headed Monsters!

Once again, the New England Patriots have turned this blogger into Al Pacino in *Godfather 3.* Every time we try to get out, they pull us back in.

This marks the second, or perhaps third, season we will not do a Patriots book on the season: main reason is economic, mostly because Patriot fans can't read and don't buy books. The other reason has to do with personal sanity.

Not since Rosey Grier and Ray Milland played one man with two heads have we seen anything as horrific. It was 1972, and the movie was *The Thing with Two Heads!*

And now Bill Belichick and Tom Brady have done the impossible: they have doubled the combustion factor on their Super Bowl team. Perhaps they like challenges, or perhaps they are fire bugs. The horrid monster of Belichick & Brady has found a mate.

Tom Brady is about to pour kerosene on top of the two most flammable players in NFL: Josh Gordon and now Antonio Brown. These Bobsey Twins could bring down governments if they were involved in Brexit.

They would be hurricanes that would defy Category 5 and find themselves the objects of Trump's madhouse White House sharpie.

Indeed, we expect a presidential tweet pardoning anyone writer who sets the tandem on a course to blow up records of pass catching and yardage.

Since Bob Kraft is owner of the Patriots, you might be a cynic and say this will permanently prove that there is no video of Kraft in a massage parlor, as it has been destroyed in an explosion of Tom Brady inflated footballs.

This makes Deflategate look like inflation pumped up to extremes that the football will look like the Goodyear Blimp in the endzone for Patriot fans.

We may now watch a few games after this Near Earth Object/asteroid crashes into Planet Foxboro.

Shot Down at the Not-Okay Corral

Many Patriot haters have waited 20 years for the moment. The parallel in history may be the Fall of the Roman Empire: the barbarians are at the gate, and Belichick and Brady are fleeing the chaos.

The Mighty Patriots have struck out. Cue Jim Morrison to sing "This is the End."

There is no joy in Mudville or Foxboro. The Pats have lost their bye week—and probably their souls.

If anyone is stunned by the Dolphins beating the Pats, you have not been paying attention. For weeks now Tom Brady has been playing like a man who will be at quarterback until he is 50—in the sandlot league.

Bill Belichick is like one of the magnificent Amberson family: he is receiving his come-uppance. His vaunted defense looked like Swiss cheese and most of his players will leave in free agency. Even Brady is expected to go out with a bang elsewhere.

History runs in cycles, and the Patriots have been top dog for a couple of decades, but now they are heading back to the rubbish pile years of the 1970s. They may spend the next two decades as outliers in the AFC.

We expect that Josh McDaniels and Julian Edelman will jump ship. Already the Florida authorities are emboldened to file new felony charges against owner Robert Kraft for human trafficking, however preposterous that seems.

Now they will feel Miami is on a roll.

On the eve of an ice storm in New England, the New England Pats may be entering a new Ice Age. The berg has hit their flank—and the unsinkable franchise has sprung a leak.

Don't cry for the Patriots, Argentina. Tom will be playing there next season.

The All-Seeing Video Eyeball

What's with video cheating and Boston's managerial brain-trusts? Their genius may be all in the eye of the camera.

We have somehow come to accept every sordid charge that Bill Belichick somehow in some way has cheated his way to win six Super Bowls. From Deflategate to Spygates 1 and 2, he seems to appear in sequels more than Rocky.

This is now the New England championship ring of truth around the world. World champs here come from the bottom of the barrel. The ring is worn on the wrong finger.

And if you had any doubt, you had only to note that now Alex Cora, winner of the 2018 World Series for the Boston Red Sox is up to his video eyeballs in cheating for both the Houston Astros and the Red Sox.

He was awarded the Sox job, it now appears, on the false pretense that he was a mastermind of winning. Well, it now appears he was indeed the mastermind—of a video spy scandal in Houston as their coach. The manager and his general manager have now been fired as a result.

Cora is hiding in plain sight. MLB states he is being investigated for making a video conference room in the Red Sox clubhouse for cheaters to view signs and other insider activities of the opposing dugout.

How long Cora stands up to this withering accusation is anyone's guess! Chances are, like Belichick, he will hunker down and figure winners never face punishment. Don't look for Cora to resign in disgrace any more than Trump will for his impeachy behaviors.

Those old interviews in which Alex Cora waxed eloquent on his admiration for Bill Belichick now take on sinister tones.

No, it will be for the true-blue Red Stockings front office to fire him. Will they? It now seems like he may fall under the New England umbrella of winners never quit and winning is the only deodorant. Managers like Casey Stengel belonged to a different century and a different club.

How Long is Shelf Life?

Josh McDaniels has been anointed. It is not quite the River Jordan, but the media has dunked Josh into the Charles River to indicate that a greater one will follow Bill Belichick.

Yes, the aimless speculation has been spurred by one particularly brain dead sports personality in Boston whose airtime is suited to an airhead.

In recent days one radio/TV simulcast show has taken the idea that the Patriots have a vice president that is waiting for President Belichick to kick the bucket.

McDaniels, now back for a second turn as offensive coordinator, has turned down head coaching jobs in a week when a dozen bad positions have opened up. As a result of Black Monday head rolling, Josh was expected to run out the door to become king of his own realm.

Instead, McDaniels told the media that he would rather be a rightful coordinator than a wrongful head coach.

No one seemed to have any evidence that Mr. Belichick was about to abdicate the throne like some lovelorn British royal.

Nevertheless, boyish Arthurian Josh McDaniels has been dubbed as the one to pull the sword from the stone and take Belichick's job. It is akin to Lancelot trying to steal the queen's affection while the king slept.

Crown prince of the Patriots is not an easy role to hold when the King has sent more princes packing over his 13-year tenure than Richard III.

No one knows (except Belichick) if the sitting king is even remotely considering an abdication.

Previous speculation has centered on Bill staying the course until his favorite consort, Tom Brady, hangs up the spikes.

What no one seems to be realizing is that when Brady retires as quarterback of the Patriots, it is he who will become its next head coach.

Nevermore and Then Some

Edgar Allen Poe left Boston and moved to Baltimore. If you believe in tracing rivalries to their source, we have the root in our grasp.

The Ravens may claim that the AFC game will nevermore allow a Patriot victory—as Brendon Ayanbadejo plays the bird this season.

Now we are engaged again in a great championship game on next Sunday.

Last season around the same time, we brought forth a playoff game, dedicated to the proposition that the Patriots were better than the Ravens.

A year later we must address the same issue once more, testing whether Patriots Nation, conceived and dedicated by Coach Bill Belichick, can long endure.

Patriots will meet on home field for that next step. Fans will come to dedicate themselves to reaching another Super Bowl. The team will dedicate their efforts to Gronk who gave so that his team could endure far beyond his power to add or to detract a new championship ring.

Foxboro is the site of the Baltimore Raven return. Fans will little note the details of the game, but they will never forget a Patriots victory of last year. It is for the players to be dedicated to the unfinished work of nobly advancing to the Super Bowl this year.

The great task remaining before the Patriots—that from Tom Brady we take increased devotion to the cause of a fourth Super Bowl ring.

The Patriots highly resolve that the Patriot Nation shall have a new Brady championship—and that the teams of Belichick, by Belichick, for the fans, will not perish in the Super Bowl.

That Poe bird faces his final caw. Nevermore, indeed.

Go, Wes. Just Go.

Bill Belichick hates Wes Welker.

You cannot deny it, Bill. The calculated plot to rid himself of a star who did not meet the cookie cutter mold that Belichick has created for his winning teams.

Welker had a public sense of humor. It turns out to be gallows humor because it has led Welker out of town, personally tarred and feathered with the worst offer ever made to a NFL receiver.

Leading the league all-time in catches from the all-star Tom Brady is no mean feat. Apparently, Coach Belichick thinks Tom can make anyone a star slot receiver.

Belichick is playing the slots with the fans' quarter— when two bits won't buy team loyalty.

You may have noticed that "won't" contains "won," which is past tense, Mr. Belichick. Shall you continue to win after dispatching your hard-playing star?

The legend that all NFL players will kill (or at least take a smaller paycheck) to play for the vaunted Belichick Genius may now be put to rest.

If your reputation starts to precede you, like a stench of death, it may be that necrosis is at the heart of your future.

If Bill Belichick wants to look fashionable on the sidelines of every game, perhaps he should pick up the ultimate hood with its scythe. Belichick has become the Patriot Grim Reaper, sending players to their fates without mercy.

A few players like Tom Brady will play chess with Belichick every night to extend his future another season, but Ingmar Bergman's *Seventh Seal* teaches us that the Grim Reaper isn't to be trusted.

The Belichick Wives

With the accusation by former Patriot Ted Johnson in regard to the wife of Vince Wilfork, informants now reveal that all Coach Bill Belichick's personnel decisions are based on the players' wives.

Ted Johnson, now a Houston Texan analyst and beauty judge, complained about Wilfork's wife, though he later apologized for wearing rose-colored glasses.

This incident has revealed the tip of the iceberg as far as the pulchritude of Patriot player wives.

Yes, Wes Welker was allowed to walk because Belichick did not like what Mrs. Welker said about Ray Lewis earlier in the season. Her subsequent apology was presumed to be too little too late.

Lately Kyle Arrington's wife has come under scrutiny from Belichick. After giving birth to a son, she has reportedly run Arrington to a frazzle with late night feedings. Belichick re-signed Arrington last week, but with a proviso that his wife had to shape up.

The only player whose wife seems to have won the Belichick beauty contest is Giselle Bundchen, wife of Tom Brady.

Skeptics claim she has won the beauty prize because she makes more money every year in modeling than all the players who sack Tom Brady combined.

In fact, she can sack Tom Brady every night to prove her value and beauty.

Patriot wives had long suspected that 'Spygate' referred to camera surveillance the Patriot coach has put on them at every game. He raised issue with players often at half-time of games when he waved photos of wives not paying attention to the defensive scheme.

Belichick reportedly approved owner Robert Kraft's new young actress girlfriend after inspecting photos taken surreptitiously at practice.

Players who are unmarried are left to the supervision of Offensive Coordinator Josh McDaniels and his cameramen.

Sessue Hayakawa

Bridge Over Troubled Waters

New England Patriots are dropping like flies onto flypaper.

The man with the paper and a list of names is Head Coach Bill Belichick who is holding his annual summer camp of tryouts. The cattle call is worse than facing the god-like Director from *A Chorus Line*, the ultimate audition show.

If you have any infraction, the voice from the rafters will call you out as unworthy to do a Texas two-step.

Belichick's corps of torture experts are driving players into early retirement if not an early grave. During the heyday of the Grand Inquisition players were put on the rack for less than Belichick wants.

Next week trials by fire and water commence. Players are already singing the main theme of *A Chorus Line*: "What I Did for Love."

Colonel Klink's Kamp was more accommodating than Generalissimo Belichick.

These summer excursions are called OTAs, a kind of voluntary trip to the underworld from where only Orpheus and Tom Brady ever return.

When the Marquis de Sade was imprisoned at the madhouse prison of Charenton, he reportedly directed a summer camp production that resembles the best work of Bill Belichick. Only in this camp we know who's running the show.

Players like Alfonzo Dennard will be the first to tell you that doing time at Boys Town Prison in Nebraska is easier than one of Belichick's reform school mastery challenges.

By the time this camp is finished, the players will march in formation and whistle a tune out of *The Bridge Over the River Kwai*, with Belichick dressed up like Sessue Hayakawa looking for a Super Bowl ring.

Godfather Hyman Belichick

A visibly nervous Bill Belichick gave perhaps the longest, most thorough explanation of process and feelings of his football coaching in his career.

The New England Patriots coach may have shocked critics by making any number of pronouncements. He tried to answer questions, mindful of the legal issues. He expressed his sorrow, his hurt, and his shock.

Following a ten-minute speech that rivaled the length of Lincoln's Gettysburg Address, the NFL coach gave an accounting that likely pleased the NFL, his ownership, his players, and the fans.

The media remained respectful in their questions—and Bill Belichick gave sober and human answers.

"This is real life," he stated about the seriousness of the case. Someone has been murdered. A family has lost a young man.

If there was any moment to stagger the mind, it was the split screen of Aaron Hernandez standing in the dock, listening to his probable cause hearing. He may as well have been hearing the words of Belichick reverberate.

Hernandez toned down his laser vision and seemed now a bit more under his counsel's advice. He wore a sport coat and remained attentive as the words of his former coach in his press conference dominated the screen. He looked grizzled and mean as usual.

The irony of the proceedings is the fact that more murder charges are in the wings. How much this affected Belichick's contrite and mournful address may not be important yet.

Suffice it to say, Bill Belichick likely changed more minds than he has ever in a hundreds of press addresses.

He had a wider stage, and he took his important big scene to play it like James Stewart in *Mr. Smith Goes to Washington*. He took on his role with all the aplomb of Lee Strasberg playing Hyman Roth in *The Godfather*.

However you rated his showmanship, Bill Belichick was compelling and gave the performance of his life.

Sensitivity Personified

The impervious Bill Belichick gave one small hint in his post-game press conference about how sensitive he really is.

Belichick noted that the Patriots did not play well in the first half of the game against the Dolphins. He mentioned off-hand that was why the fans were booing as they went off the field.

What on earth is this? Bill Belichick is responding to a poll of public opinion? Apparently the coach knows when people are displeased with him and his team's effort.

Not surprisingly, upon returning to the field, the Patriots looked like the team of yore—minus many of their biggest stars. This is the new-fangled, Belichick Laboratories' creation.

The mad scientist of the NFL has been concocting winners for years, and this year he went back to the recipe book for something new and not as sweet. Alas, his soufflé has fallen flat on a weekly basis, but at halftime against the Dolphins, a dollop of dolphin fish oil seems to have done the trick.

The Patriots then gave the fans a treat.

Knuckles Brady denied his edema of the fist had any effect on his game. Though some worried he should not have been playing, we saw Belichick come to the sidelines and speak some sweet nothing at his star. Tom gave a cursory nod and played like a man ten years younger.

Purists may decry the state of the Patriots, but if your record says who you are, this is a team that may not look pretty, but they are compiling wins however they can gather them.

Ebenezer Belichick

Following in the shoes of his teammate Alfonzo Dennard who pleaded no contest to DUI in Nebraska this week, Stevan Ridley is pleading no contest to DUF (dropping unnecessarily f*****s).

Our intrepid stringer Charles Dickens sent in this report:

The hanging judge in this case is the warm-hearted Bill Belichick, always filled with the season's giving at this time of year.

When Stevan came to make his case, Belichick merely asked Ridley, "Are there no workhouses?"

Ridley answered, "All too many." Little Stevan made his case, "At this time of year some players suffer greatly."

Belichick snarled, "Are there no fumbles?"

Ridley cried, "Plenty of fumbles."

Belichick was undaunted: "And is the Players Union still in operation?"

Stevan noted, "They are very busy at this time of year, dealing with bad officiating."

The Patriots coach snickered, "Oh, I was afraid from what you said at first something had occurred to remove them from impeding my justice system."

The star running back lamented, "Will you allow me to put down the ball on the sidelines and hold one in the game?"

"You wish to play then? Since you ask me, I don't play myself, and I can't afford to lose games at this time of year. If you are so badly off, maybe you should play for the Jets."

"Many won't go there, and many others would rather die."

"Then don't drop the ball or you will decrease the population of the 53-man roster."

Seeing it was useless to pursue a case with Belichick, Ridley grabbed his football and tucked it under his arm.

As he left the coach's office, he could hear the words, "It's enough for a man to understand how to carry a football. That's your business. Now, my business is to win games and it occupies me totally."

Ridley did not let the door hit him on the way out.

Covenant of the Ark

As far as we can tell, Bill Belichick has not begun to build an ark. Rain in Foxboro during January is a good thing, though Belichick has two of every position on his team. He needed a spare for nearly every job.

As the deluge fell upon Andrew Luck, he seemed wet behind the ears. Believers would say he likes to play with the handicap of being two touchdowns down.

The wonder of this playoff game was that Tom Brady threw no touchdowns before his time. This was a team effort with blockers and runners like Stevan Ridley and LaGarrette Blount's four scores.

If Blount can run like this with four scores every game, it could add seven years to Tom Brady's career.

The Patriots looked like a team of destiny that had saved all its good luck for the post-season, while Luck looked like he had run out it.

The Patriots won this game the old fashioned way. They earned it.

Can it be that Bill Belichick finally wants to prove that he doesn't need Brady? Of course, it is more diabolical than that. The next team won't know whether they will get Tom Jekyll, master passer, or Hyde Brady, the man who lets them run.

At season's start we never expected that the names synonymous with victory would be names we never gave much thought to.

Like all classic champions, the Patriots have saved the best for last. With games dwindling down to a precious few, the Pats have righted the ship.

Belichick's Folly

New England Patriot diva and hermit cookie, Bill Belichick, now adds the Greta Garbo Award to his litany of achievements.

Like the mercurial movie star of the Golden Age, Bill Belichick has disdained his fellow coaches and expressed his wishes to be left alone.

Coach Bill Belichick went to the NFL Coaches Association meeting and declined to be in their group photo. He later opined that they could 'Photoshop' him into the image.

This was heady stuff from a man who doesn't know a Facebook page from his Tweets.

After seeing the NFL coaches gathered together in a variety of moo=moos and Hawaiian shirts, we can understand why Belichick took a powder. Not one coach had the good taste to wear cut-off sleeves or a hoodie.

We are certain Belichick's feelings would have been hurt had he not been invited to say, "Cheese." Even if you never attend an event, it's always nice to be asked.

In recent years Belichick has jousted with the media enough to earn the sobriquet as Heidi's Other Grandfather. Now he is anathema to his own kind: the looney association of obsessed megalomaniac football coaches.

These are the men who make self-importance a virtue. And, now they have been outdone by the Zen master of Lone Ranger head coaches.

Belichick may have left a silver bullet as he rode off on his white charger, yelling, "Hi-Yo, Welker."

Belichick has now stiffed everyone who did not send him a Christmas Card this year. It was his Hallmark moment to scoff at media events that are condoned by the League of Gentlemen that pays him.

Run, Bill, Run!

Bill Belichick did in his off-season what he never could do in Boston in any season. He ran a half-marathon on the cusp of retirement age. He had to go to a place where no one seems to know his name to avoid the Cheers crowd.

Yes, the Old Hoodie did not need a hoodie to hide his face as he ran half the distance to the NFL Draft while he was in Nashville, Tennessee, for the Music City Half-Marathon.

The Boston Marathon is twice as long as the old coach cares to run, and if he chose to run in Boston, they'd need armed guards and mammoth security to protect him. Come to think of it: the Boston Marathon could have offered him more protection than he needed this year.

With a brigade of detractors of the fit as a fiddle head coach of the New England Patriots, Belichick managed to run the Nashville race in a little more than two and a half hours. In full marathon regalia, he'd have crossed the Boylston Street Finish Line shortly before dusk.

Belichick ran like a man running away from the hordes of media that gum up his running track at Gillette Stadium every week of the season, or maybe he used Wes Welker as inspiration.

What makes Bill run? You'd need Budd Schulberg to figure it out, but he has certainly proven that he can outlast Tom Brady when it comes to longevity.

A couple of years ago former Patriot Steve DeOssie ran the Boston Marathon in conjunction with a PBS documentary about the difficulty of performing such a competition.

This year one of Bill Belichick's darlings, Tedy Bruschi, decided to run the Marathon. We are sure that Bill would not have been alone if he had chosen to run part of the course in Boston.

Zombieland

Something is rotten in the state of Foxboro.

We haven't quite seen Hamlet's Ghost, but it is starting to look like the Ghost of Past, Present, and Future Super Bowls may be making a call and throwing a yellow flag.

Patriots experts said there would be a massacre against Rex Ryan's deplorable Jets on a Thursday night, but the truth was stranger. The Jets almost pulled a victory out of the humble pie like it was a plum.

The Walking Dead aren't just a cable TV show. They are the army of former Patriots and injured Patriots that have been sent to Zombieland by Bill Belichick.

The latest hobbling zombies are Stevan Ridley and Jerod Mayo. It's a dill pickle indeed. Throw in Logan

Mankins and Wes Welker and you have the cold slawing of the Patriots.

We hasten to point out that the next few weeks will mean a curtain call for the season. The strongest opponents outside of playoff time will be knock-knock-knocking on heaven's door and Belichick's defense.

The Patriots have played well against the worst, and they may lose every game against the best.

With the Celtics, Red Sox, and Bruins, now flirting with closing the lid on the toilet, the Patriots seemed to be the only ones on automatic flush. Now we suspect they may not make it to the potty in a knick of time.

After several seasons of gloating about good times, the floodgates of losing are wide open. And, our little Boston boat is about to be swamped. Somewhere Aaron Hernandez is laughing.

Chance of Rain

When it rains, it pours. At least that is the problem that Bill Belichick faces every week. He thinks Tom Brady can outpass the Weather Channel.

And if it isn't raining, it's too windy. But, no one can create a gust of windbag proportions more than the man who terrorizes Suzy Snowflake every winter.

In one of the most brazen attacks on his opponents in his career, Bill Belichick proved he was no fair weather fan.

He blasted the standard opponents as being so wrongfully constituted that they went cold half-way through any game.

Though a team named Meteorologists is not on the docket for the Super Bowl, Belichick may want to save his true fire and brimstone for a cold, winter, outdoor game. If he dismisses these weather guys now, he will be on Cloud 9 in February.

Bill Belichick has become a true New Englander. He realizes that Mark Twain was right. If you don't like the weather, just wait a minute. It will change.

The New England Patriots coach often is a weathervane for fans and other NFL teams. As Bob Dylan said of Belichick, he's blowing in the wind. And then some. Now he is a beacon on the rocky shores of New England, alerting us to bad weather forecasts.

Belichick became bellicose when his favorite NFL opponent's fickle nature was raised. He then raised the roof beams with one of his most loquacious tirades and rants about weather people forecasting like amateurs.

Everybody complains about the weather, but Bill Belichick is prepared to do something about it.

Game conditions look downright mercurial on Sunday. According to Belichick, it will be sunny and pleasant.

Witnesses Unleashed: Belichick & Spikes

At long last the real reason Brandon Spikes was sent packing has been revealed.

When the Patriots let Brandon Spikes go to the Buffalo Bills, you had to wonder what was behind the conflict with Coach Bill Belichick.

We know Belichick is not a man to be crossed, and he is a man who crosses his Ts and eliminates any extraneous uncrossed Ts. Brandon Spikes was a thorn in his side. And, he knew too much.

Now that the Aaron Hernandez witness, witless list is public, we find that Belichick and Spikes share an unpleasant tie: *confidantes* of said serial killer Hernandez.

Whatever Belichick said or did with Hernandez, the killer likely told his old college buddy, Spikes. Those Florida boys learned early how to cheat and get away with it. And, Belichick seemed to find them irresistible. He even brought Tim Tebow in for a while for comic relief.

Spikes will have plenty of time to testify during the trial, as his season will be long over by the time his subpoena arrives. Belichick, on the other hand, will be in the midst of preparing his game plans for a February super day.

Spikes thinks nothing of shooting off his mouth, and Belichick is the epitome of laconic. Somewhere with the prosecuting attorneys, these two must have crossed wires.

Some speculate that the "safe house" where Hernandez stored his guns and drugs was an idea given him by a far smarter adviser. That isn't Spikes. The adviser probably isn't owner Robert Kraft who readily admits he is a dupe of the first order.

We can hardly wait for trial time. And remember, folks, there will be two trials. You can be sure if Belichick's testimony is juicy, the prosecutors for the subsequent double-homicide will be licking their chops.

Into the Cauldron

Double, double toil and trouble.

That evil genius of the NFL had his cauldron on full bubble during the Saturday playoff game.

Bill Belichick threw in an eye of newt into the mix, which apparently had the effect of driving Ravens coach John Harbaugh into parboil mode.

Feeling it was a trick, though he carefully avoided calling it cheating or a dirty trick, the Raven coach clearly felt that the Patriots had done something never seen before on a football field.

It was a death knell for the Ravens. It was an act nevermore to be tolerated. It left the dirty bird lying prostrate on Foxboro field.

The larks were singing, but the ravens had turned into just another minor bird.

Macbeth's witches had nothing on Belichick and his second in command warlock, Josh McDaniel and the war-gronk in training, Gronk.

They offered the Ravens a Super Bowl ring, but could only be stopped by a team led by a man not of woman born. Belichick never revealed his roots of being hatched in a laboratory.

Not only were the substitutions from hell, but Belichick the Ripper had failed quarterback Julian Edelman throw a touchdown pass to failed receiver Danny Amendola.

It torched the Ravens worse than Burnham wood torched Macbeth. Thrice and once, the hedge pig whin'd. Suggs was a fillet of fenny snake, and Harbaugh was panting with a tongue of dog.

You might expect baboon's blood in a game like this, but clearly Shakespeare had it all over Poe in this game. Add block

Addressing the Playoffs

If you ask haters of Bill Belichick, they will tell you that he lives under a rock.

A recent appearance at a press conference during playoff season proved he lives in his office. Disheveled and grizzled, the Patriot coach looks like a man who prefers flattened cardboard boxes to a box spring.

Belichick never leaves the stadium during this pivotal time of the year. Satan also never sleeps in other breaking news.

The reason for Belichick's success is his dedication, albeit obsession, to his job. There is no time for a meal when you are plotting the upset of the NFL world. Though Patriot Place next to the stadium features comfy hotel rooms and trendy restaurants, Belichick prefers Boston baked beans, preferably eaten cold out of a can with a plastic spoon.

There can be no frills when the honor of a man mostly despised and dishonored is facing another chance at redemption. Lately he has come back to his office after a Super Bowl all the poorer and more dedicated to his air mattress.

You'd think this man would buy a memory foam mattress, but Bill Belichick doesn't need memory foam. He never forgets a loss. And he won't sleep on it.

He is now engaged in a great NFL war, and you can count on the fact that old Bill will endure. If sleeping on a cold floor is a test of his dedication, Belichick will make Gillette Stadium his final resting place if there are no more Super Bowl rings.

Living out of his office, Belichick plans his unfinished work. His players will not play in vain. He will give his last full measure of devotion to bring a Super Bowl victory to the people of New England.

Rounding Up Twice the Usual Shocks

If you felt like you were watching a bad remake of the Humphrey Bogart classic, *Casablanca,* you were not alone.

The Bill Belichick press conference about Deflategate seemed to be re-enacting one of the more famous scenes of the movie.

The *gendarmes* crash into Rick's Place for a raid. Whistles blow and everyone scrambles.

Bogart demands to know what is going on from the Prefect of police, Captain Renault. As played by the slick Claude Rains, his expression is purely feigned innocence.

Captain Renault barks out, "I am shocked, shocked, shocked, to hear there is gambling going on in this establishment."

Rick storms away in fury, and one of the *croupiers* runs up to Captain Renault and hands him his winnings, which he promptly stuffs into his pocket. "Oh, thank you."

Bill Belichick gave his press conference and noted duly with a straight face, "I am shocked, shocked, shocked to hear that footballs were under-inflated." The first he heard of this was Monday morning when he came into his office at 4am.

Belichick had never in his life ever discussed the psi of footballs with anyone. In fact, he simply plays the game with the equipment given him at game time.

He never questions the inflation of the balls, the atmospheric pressure of the stadium, or the meteorologist's forecast of the game.

Yes, indeed, we are shocked, shocked, shocked!

OK Humor

The old gunslinger came out with his pistols blazing.

Bill Belichick mowed down the press with all the aplomb of Clint Eastwood in a spaghetti Western. We have not seen such fire-breathing vengeance in a dozen seasons from Bill.

Usually Just Plain Bill talks like a man with a prolonged case of dyspepsia expecting more hot sauce in his diet. On this Saturday, a week before the Super Bowl, he came across as a man whose homemade chili just burned out his esophagus.

Up an octave, down a reporter, he took down those who raised cheatgate, Spygate, and deflategate with a flurry of piercing blue-eyed laser beams.

Among the hastily drawn media crowd, those who asked rude questions ought to know they only lived by the grace of Bill Belichick. But, their names, ranks, and serial numbers, were duly noted.

Belichick announced he had conducted his own investigation, and he dared anyone there to snicker.

If Randolph Scott told the assembled town meeting that he was going to restore law and order to the West, you knew he meant business in one of those 1950s hard-boiled Westerns he did as precursor to Clint.

Belichick has had to waste his precious time bringing law and order to the Super Bowl—and now he was ready for the big showdown. It wasn't going to be at noon near Tombstone, Arizona. He was putting the world on notice that "them varmints" who disrespect the Patriots ought to get out of town by sunset, February 1st.

The OK Corral has just been moved to Glendale, Arizona, and Patriot detractors better head for the hills. Belichick is on the warpath.

One Thin Dime

Just wait one flipping minute.

Have we read the tweet correctly? There are NFL officials who believe the New England Patriots are winning too many coin tosses.

Can it be that Bill Belichick has a coach on his staff whose expertise is voodoo? We wonder too if there is a voodoo doll of Roger Goodell at Patriot Place with pins sticking in its head.

Was P.T. Barnum wrong? Is it possible you can underestimate the intelligence of the American sports fan? We are amazed that coin flipping, a time-tested method of 50-50 probability, has now been questioned by the same people who scored a 2 on their Wonderlic tests.

The Wonderlic test now must require a question of how many sides are there on a coin! Answers may be one, two, three, four, or all of the above.

If we recall correctly, the referee shows both sides of the coin to the team captains at the game's onset. We now wonder if team captains can tell the difference between heads and tails. With the fancy new designs on coins, perhaps they don't know the difference.

It is possible that these team captains have actually never seen a coin because they pay for everything with credit cards—or their smartphones.

Is it any wonder that Bill Belichick prefers not to be known as the Wizard of Gillette Stadium? Please tell us: who is that man standing behind the curtain in the technology booth?

Roger Goodell is collecting all the silver dollars used this season for coin tosses. Smart man.

You can expect a congressional hearing soon on Flipping-gate.

Paper Chase and Media Beater

Bill Belichick disdained his midterm report card.

You'd think the head coach of the New England Patriots would gladly accept accolades and A's for his efforts this season.

This is not your twin brother's Rex Ryan. Belichick sneered with more alacrity than usual when some dopey media person asked what grade he deserved as a coach at mid-season.

Bill does not suffer fools gladly—and press conferences seem to test his pedal to the mettle. These cub reporters never learn their lessons enough to receive more than a failing grade. Professor Belichick never gives multiple guess tests.

Responding with all the ever-acerbic zeal of Bill Parcells, Mr. Belichick thought the idea of a mid-season grade went out with *summa cum laude.* He eschewed any grading system as worse than pass/fail.

Under the circumstances, he noted that he deserved an F.

Football is not the first semester of college—despite what FanDuel or DraftKings may tell you. And Bill Belichick is the Professor Kingsfield of the media chase and Super Bowl graduate school. If he has a seating plan for reporters and media geeks at his weekly presser, he knows what maroon to call on for the worst question.

One of these days he will hand a reporter a dime and tell him to call his mother and say he failed out of Football 101.

Unlike bombastic Rex Ryan who only circles the games with the Patriots on his schedule, Bill Belichick never circles anything. He is more of a rhomboid guy. And, there is no neutral corner.

Back to the Abacus

As Bill Belichick now must deal with the worst decision of his coaching career, he has taken to justifying it. Talk about making matters worse. He claims he was making a list and checking it twice when the infamous coin flip seems to have flipped him a bird.

The diabolical Hoodie of yore would never have stood on the sidelines, playing with his etch-a-sketch, which some commentators have mistakenly called an iPad.

Everyone knows Roger Goodell has made a $400 million deal with the famous toymaker to give coaches something under their Xmas tree. The blue bauble appears to have no Internet connectivity, let alone an off switch.

It was on this little blue tablet, often called a Surface at Microsoft, that the New England braintrust seems to have drawn up one of the worst plans of the regular season.

The NFL Etch has no memory, no statistics, and no known reasonable function. Yet, Belichick used it to decide to kick a ball to the Jets in overtime, thereby giving them a chance to score instantly.

Technophobes like Belichick then could use the device to prove that *Steve Jobs* was a bad movie about knock-offs.

Since Belichick's defensive schemers were unable to stop the March of the Jet Toy Soldiers, the Etch-a-Sketch turned Tom Brady into Betsy Wetsy. Matt Patricia, the erstwhile Defensive Coordinator, was degraded to using #2 pencils to work it out.

It seemed like the Jets took the old-fashioned Slinky hop and bounce over the Patriots D-men.

It appears that the motto, "In Bill We Trust," has been deflated.

Blessed are the Playmakers

Insiders are reporting that the Great Hoodie of Gillette City has decided to keep his ruby red slippers under wraps.

He gave nothing away in the last few games of the season when double agents, scouts, and media spies are looking for a report to help plan a strategy to defeat the New England team. What they saw likely created overconfidence and arrogance.

It has rattled athletic supporters on the home front jewels.

Once again, Coach Bill Belichick let them eat cake. And, they will starve to death on that special diet of rotten apples and stale crackers, compliments of the Great Hoodie.

There was nothing obvious in what tactics the Patriot coaches will take in the playoffs. This Belichick *soup du jour* is diabolical and brilliant.

Film and game plans are oft created by watching the performances and player groupings of your opponent. If they watched the Patriots in December, they learned nothing. It was not a month to remember.

In the past Belichick has relied on the notion that the brains of his next opponent are focused, like a fly, on the recent weeks of play, and they never look much beyond it with their goldfish memories.

But Belichick is like the elephantine wizard dominating the room. He recalls all, and he knows all. What he has shown to the potential adversaries in the playoffs is that his team is weak, injured, and the coaches are slipping. What a brilliant façade.

It is the ultimate Potemkin village. When the opponents drive by in their sleighs, thinking it's a holiday, he will pounce with guerilla aplomb.

You can bet the practices over the next two weeks will have more security than Homeland provides the Congress. That is the telltale heart of Belichick at work.

Shiner of Shiners

Who killed Cock Robin? And who slugged Bill Belichick?

Belichick showed up this week with a need to list himself on the IR (injured reserve) list. He is injured, and he is reserved. But, Bill is the first to tell you coaches don't have to report.

When inquiries came his way, he gave an answer worthy of a Clint Eastwood script, "I think I'll live."

If you want more than that, you will carted off by Patriot security forces. No one dared to ask.

We'd need Hercule Poirot and Miss Marple to team up to solve this mystery.

We suspect Colonel Mustard in the film room with the Etch-a-Sketch that Bill always works out strategies upon. More unlikely to blame is Aaron Hernandez. He has a built-in alibi, being shut in prison. Besides, his *modus operandi* would be gun at close range.

The chief witness and alleged victim is not talking, as per usual.

However, Coach Bill Belichick was in mid-week form early when he came to his press conference with a black eye, daring the assembled multitude of cowards to speak up.

Giving black eyes is the purview of the NFL—but we were intrigued at what player socked Bill in the eye socket. And, more importantly, what did he say and do to deserve such treatment?

As one of the major rumor mongers and alarmists in all New England, we want to be the first to cause an uproar and make false accusations.

Was it an over-inflated football to the face in the head?

Like Norma Desmond, Belichick was not ready for his closeup—and local media did not zero in on a lumpish mess above his left eye. Film may be at eleven, but only after Bill turns in for the night.

Media Attack Belichick!

Bill Belichick may have come to the end of the line with the media.

Never one to share much information about his strategies or plans to replace injured players, he has gone completely 'stonewall' on the Jimmy G issue.

Even during Watergate, Nixon never had as much *chutzpah* as Belichick.

All the best attributes of Belichick have been put into the center of his universe after losing Jimmy G—and the wagons have been circled. If Custer had been as cognizant of the enemy, he would never have met his demise at Little Big Horn.

And, those press conferences with the Boston, New England, United States, world media, have now become an attack from 6 billion Indians who want his scalp.

General George Armstrong Belichick has lost his replacement QB—and media moguls are asking if he will bring back Tim Tebow (who once labored in Foxboro for few short weeks) to handle the one and a half games before the nuclear weapon of Tom Brady is released from its missile silo.

Someone should tell Belichick to stop worrying and learn how to love the bomb, or at least someone should have the courage to tell him to watch the hoary Kubrick movie, *Dr. Strangelove.* Belichick is starting to raise his arm too often in a habitual salute to his own sense of victory.

Like his pal Donald Trump, Belichick will never apologize for making the Patriots great. It's easy to see that in Coach Belichick's world, the loss of Jimmy G is tantamount to the Great White Shark in *Jaws* breaking one of his teeth.

Another new tooth will pop up from the row of teeth in waiting below the gum line.

Jacoby B's Line

The yellow-streaked rose of the Texans is shining in New England. The Houston Texans looked as bad as Governor Rick Perry on *Dancing with the Stars* in their Foxboro appearance.

It's threaten the Patriots QB time. This week Texan J.J. Watt is promising to bury Jacoby Brissett. However, we couldn't find Watt on the field, but we surely saw much of Jacoby B. He played with the pizzazz usually reserved for Jimmy G.

Gronk played in a game for the first time this season, but he looked like the gray ghost in blue.

The Patriots seemed alive with new names: Hogan and Logan amused us, but not nearly as much as seeing former old Patriots all over the Houston team: Wilfork, Izzo, Vrable, Romeo, O'Brien, and on and on. It was deju woo woo.

NFL players know the league will let them dance on the graves of the Patriots with impunity. Thank you, Goddell. The referees seemed intent on giving the game to Houston on every close call—and Belichick seemed unmotivated to fight it (he won one challenge), but will accept the ugly fate of the NFL—only to still beat the enemy.

All of this was done with the bad luck blue-on-blue uniforms that we heard Bill Belichick loathes. Every time they wear these, the Pats lose. However, disgust over not having Tom on the team likely negated this superstition.

We were delighted when Chum maker Nate Ebner, rugby Olympian, caused a fumble. Among the Texan problems were several fumbles, an interception, pass interference in the end zone, and odd coaching.

If ever Tom Brady wanted to stick it to the NFL front office, he saw the third game without his star going supernova.

Dropping a Dime on Bill

Bill Belichick has been compared to Napoleon, but his real diabolical nature when it comes to football scandals truly makes him the "Napoleon of Crime."

His detractors would say he lives on the edge of honesty, likely to be seduced by the twisting of rules. Like the first Napoleon of Crime, he never sullies his own hands in accomplishing his goals.

Of course, the first Napoleon of Crime was Sherlock Holmes's truly despicable opponent, Professor Moriarty. Any resemblance between Bill Belichick and an academic is more acutely like Professor Kingsfield, of *Paper Chase* lore. Kingsfield notably told off students. "Here is a dime. Call your mother and tell her you will never be a real sports journalist."

There is not a strategy, tactic, or moral beyond Belichick Napoleon when it comes to manipulating his players. They are mere clay to be molded to his laser beam focus. And this week, the nemesis of the Napoleon of Crime will be the amateur sleuthing brothers of prepubescent lore—the Ryan Brothers, or as their match in literary terms—the Hardy Boys.

It hardly seems fair to pit the disingenuous Hardy Boys against the nefarious Napoleon of Crime, but it does seem apt. Rex and Rob Ryan have a refreshing innocence when it comes to facing up to intimidation from Swami Belichick.

Some astute observers might say those Ryan Brothers are little David going up against Goliath.

If Belichick used his talents to do crime, he probably would abscond with the Mona Lisa out of the Louvre museum unimpeded. As it is, he will likely score 30 points unimpeded against the Ryan Boys.

Even without a QB, Belichick's team will be formidable. After all, he is showing the world that he does not need Tom Brady to flatten the landscape in the AFC East.

Technophobe

Bill Belichick has rejected use of the Surface, a Microsoft version of the iPad for in-game, on-field usage.

The grumpy old man of football has given all those post-60 types cause to celebrate dumping tea into Boston Harbor. Yes, we saw Swami Bill smash his tablet during a game a few weeks ago. Now he has tossed his tablet into the harbor as a form of protest.

We were reminded of Moses smashing the tablets he brought down from the mountain for similar reasons. It was hard to get a handle on them.

Of course, Microsoft has responded with more than a bit of shock that the greatest coach in the NFL today has tossed out their product as unreliable. It seems they need an aspirin tablet after failing to live up to Swami Belichick's high standard.

Younger types might snicker at the old reprobate turned technophobe, but purists will take pictures over fancy screen words every time.

The Patriots head coach didn't just reject tablets with a wave of the hand. The laconic Belichick who never has words for any occasion, devoted five minutes to run down the notion as, "I have given them as much time as I can give them."

Wow, this ought to make Stephen Gostowski worry about his next missed point-after.

Belichick went on to dun all technology—from headsets to the abacus. "Those fail on a regular basis. There are very few games that we play, home or away, day, night, cold , hot preseason, regular, season, postseason where there aren't issues in some form or fashion with the equipment." Talk about taking a broad brush in a high handed fashion.

In short, Bill Belichick has moved on from the 21stcentury technology. He is on to the Stone Age. And our fellow Neanderthals love it.

Nearer to Thy Maker in Pittsburgh

Pitts-aburger has lost its Rothlisberger for the Patriots game. Hold that ketchup.

Mere mortals might worry that their team was in jeopardy of losing to the Brady Vindication Tour, but not those meatheads from Pittsburgh.

The Steelers have lost their quarterback for this game—and the Patriots have lost their iPad knockoffs. In far worse news, Wednesday was the last day to register to vote in the upcoming MMA bout between Trump and Clinton.

The NFL marquee matchup has lost its luster. You saw more action in the 21st century version of the Lincoln-Douglas debacle debate between the Trumpeter and the Hildebeest.

ESPN, the alleged network that made up Deflategate, now claims the Patriots are dirtier than a presidential campaign, asserting the Pats play is dirtiest in NFL. Do these guys ever watch games?

How worried is Swami Bill? This week, historical for those nasty debates and a charity dinner that Clinton and Trump turned most uncharitable, also marked the longest pregame press conference ever held by the Head Coach.

Yup, the laconic HC turned loquacious for once. He even extended his required NFL time with the press because he was feeling so wordy. His staff tried to pull him off-stage, but Bill stayed with the ones he loved: his media buds. He took a couple of additional questions.

If he wanted to portray an air of ease and charm, he came off like a tanned and rested Richard Nixon. He talked football history and coaches he admired. It was enough to send shivers into Pittsburgh.

If Belichick had lit up a Red Auerbach (the legendary Celtics coach always puffed on a stogie before the final buzzer when he felt confident) victory Cuban cigar at the podium, it would have had the same effect.

In the immortal words of Alfred E. Neumann, "What? Me worry?"

Inscrutable Bill

Once again during a bye week, Patriots fans have taken umbrage with our terms of endearment.

Apparently it is just short of sacrilege to call Bill Belichick by the Hindu term "swami."

Some people (of less than sharp mental acuity) have confused swami with Swanee. No, we are not comparing Bill Belichick to a Stephen Foster melody. He is not like a pretty girl.

Those who live in the Boston area and drive over the Mystic River Bridge likely have a better grasp on the term "Swami Bill."

And, no, it has nothing to do with receiving a bill for your tolls over the Mystic River.

To clarify, we might compare Swami Bill to Yogi Berra—or Yogi Bear.

They seem to be cut from the same sari cloth worn by fashion-plates like Harry Krishna.

For all you Dharma Bums, Bill Belichick seems to be holding on to some kind of satori, having epiphanies when it comes to player personnel. We have not yet put Bill Belichick into the marharishi category. We haven't seen any pilgrimages by Lord Paul McCartney to the Foxboro mountain top. No, Bon Jovi doesn't count.

We do know that the High Lama is named Brady, and the code word for Gillette is Shangri-La.

We are not even sure that Belichick has emulated Kerouac and written the road play book on a continuous roll of toilet paper. You wouldn't understand it anyhow.

If you don't know what's going on with the Patriots, you are no Swami Bill.

Patriotic Gore?

It was politics as usual in the Patriots locker room.

No one wanted to talk about President-Elect Donald Trump's boast that both Swami Belichick and Tommy B were big supporters of the future president. The Super Patriots are putting a focus on the Big Game, not the Big Election.

Patriots to a man claimed that wanted to beat Pete Carroll on Sunday, not Hillary Clinton on Tuesday. They may have a double-header victory.

Tom Brady told a radio interview he had not yet voted on Monday—meaning he skipped the chance to cast a ballot early in Massachusetts, if indeed he is a registered resident voter of New England. He could be on the roster for California.

Brady has a cap in his locker that reads, "Make New England great again!"

On the other hand, Swami Bill Belichick had been blind-sided by his presidential friend. He had written a letter of support to the Donald, which he thought was private. He should have known better than to send Trump an e-mail.

Belichick learned there are no national secrets. He may control New England and the Kraft family, but he was trumped by the new president.

At first, the reaction against them was like an Elizabeth Warren hurricane, but now in the light of victory, they are looking like Super Bowl champs.

Sen. Warren, a vocal terror of Trumpers, now may face another Boston sports legend, Curt Schilling, who wants to run against her. We suspect the Trump victory will go far in encouraging him to unseat the Native American claimant.

All this political stuff has begun to make patriotic Patriot fans feel like strange bedfellows.

Drive, He Said

Local jokesters ribbed each other yesterday by saying Swami Belichick might claim drunk driver Michael Floyd. Today, the laughingstock is taking stock of another brilliant Belichick move.

Yes, the Patriots have signed a public relations disaster. No, he is not quite in the league of Johnny Manziel. This is more like Floyd Boyzeal.

Drunk drivers never walk a straight line in football. They best catch the ball and zigzag. Former Patriot coach Charlie Weis was Floyd's college coach at Notre Dame and suspended the player for DUI. So, he gave Belichick a rousing report that may sound like a drinking dirge.

Swami Bill usually works some magic on the bad boys of football, causing them to walk the straight and narrow while singing the Great Hoodie's praises.

How odd indeed that a solid player (a hale and hardy saloon patron) is suddenly free in December for the Patriots to scoop up. It smacks of LaGarrett Blount being tossed into the rubbish heap two years ago—just in time to pull the Patriots' bacon out of the fire.

Far be it for us to deflate any bubbleheads, but this is the sort of maneuver that pays dividends around Super Bowl time when your best receivers are on the injured list.

So, Belichick's Salvation Army of Patriot reclamation projects will gather around Michael Floyd and sing a few bars of "Amazing Grace" to bring him to sobriety and success.

Whether we are about to view *Miracle on Foxboro Street*, or you are about to see Belichick's version of Apple Annie revert to a *Pocketful of Miracles*, only the next few weeks will prove.

Like *It's a Wonderful Life,* Belichick is about to help Michael Floyd earn his wings. Yep, this is the Great Hoodie version of turning wino into water boy.

Winner, Take All

The Patriots celebrated Christmash and the AFC East, on a Saturday afternoon by devastating the New York Jets.

If it were a boxing match, it would have been called because of too frequent nosebleeds from the rainy day New Yawkers.

The Patriots rained on the parade of Jets during the first half. When they were all wet, the rains of Ranchipur and Foxboro relented, but the mercy was too late.

Tom Brady was waving up to his visiting Brazilian in-laws after one touchdown, and LaGarrette Blount was holding a cape for the waiting Martellus Bennett after the next.

When Bennett came to the sidelines, he seemed delighted that Blount was holding the robe to drape over the shoulders of the tight end who would be Gronk.

The Patriots put 41 lumps on coal into the Jets stocking, just in time for deflating the Macy Parade animals. For this loss, coach Todd Bowles released himself from the hospital the day before—and came to the downpours to stand there like Rick waiting for Ilsa at the train station in *Casablanca.*

Victory was not going to show up for the Jets this day.

It was a day when Belichick's *Bell, Book, and Candle,* were not going to be exorcised. It was a holiday when crowds cheered the DUI Michael Floyd who caught a ball out of bounds and received an ovation.

Gronk brought his charity lottery winner to the game to watch from the luxury boxes. And, in the second half, the skies miraculously cleared and bright sunlight shone down upon the blessed Patriots.

Yes, December would end with division championships and home field advantage. Their rivals saw their QBs bite the dust in Oakland and Tennessee, but youthful Tom Brady was standing tall, casting a dark shadow on Roger Goodell.

The Super Bowl seemed within Brady's grasp for this year.

Avoiding Witness Stand

While deliberations of the jury entered the fifth day, reports came forth that Jose Baez did indeed try to subpoena New England's head coach, Bill 'Don't Call Me Swami' Belichick.

We learned that old Belichick has the speed and agility of a young Dak Prescott by managing with guile, speed, and legal talent, to avoid the process servers of Baez.

Apparently Baez is not too smart when it comes to finding someone to serve his summons. Reporters have been able to find Belichick everywhere since the season ended, including the front row of the parquet at Boston Garden for a Celtics game.

Alas, they could not reach Belichick. His armed guards must be better at blocking the enemy than Tom Brady's linemen.

NFL law means never having to answer to a court summons. So, Belichick called Judge Jeffrey Locke to see if there were any ramifications in avoiding testimony.

Baez thought he did not finally need Belichick. He seems confident that Hernandez will walk away from the double-murder charge.

Feeling above the law, Belichick gave an interview just five days ago in which he called the Hernandez case "a tragedy" and "heartbreaking." Yeah, it breaks your heart and bank account when you pay a serial killer $40 million buckeroos—and he starts to shoot people who spill a drink on his clean shirt.

We might think something more profound in its shock might be the coach's response, but we have learned that from the Pouncey brothers and their "Free Aaron" hats to actual teammates of Hernandez, most NFL participants have no thoughts about a sports version of Jack the Ripper.

Normal people might be indignant at the lack of understanding among athletes when they harbor and protect a killer. It lends the most horrific credence to the amorality of Belichick's team and the NFL in general.

Yes, We Have No Bananas

Did Bill Belichick just put a razor blade in Patriot fans' apple? Or like the serpent in the Garden of Eden, did he simply offer the Apple to the Sodom and Gomorrah team of America?

Shock waves continue to reverberate around New England as the man in the Grim Reaper costume goes door to door, locker to locker, looking for another trick to pull.

Tom Brady, youthful optimist, wished another of his long-term second-bananas the best of luck. Poor Jimmy

G will need it with the band of merry losers out by the Golden Gate.

The revolving door of quarterbacks likely means that Belichick has another sleight of hand at the ready before the end of trade deadline. We are not privy to the inner machinations of the Machiavelli of football.

We would suggest that Drew Bledsoe will not come out of retirement for the Patriots. Their last-ditch quarterback replacement always was Julian Edelman who is now wearing his costume for the big Day of the Dead festival in Foxboro.

We already let the black cat out of the bag before tossing him into the Charles River by mentioning the name of Brian Hoyer, long-time Shemp to the stooges who wait in vain for Brady to grow old.

Brady is smiling like Alfred E. Neumann because he knows that he will never age and will never lose a step.

Does Robert Kraft have Colin Kaepernick's smarts?

God Bless Those Steelers Too

Back like the Macy Parade or Peewee Herman for another holiday special, Bill Belichick will host the grandest Xmas party on the streaming web, as in previous jolly seasons.

Unfortunately, only those with access to the DarkNet will be able to download this journey to the dark-side of Christmas in Pittsburgh.

Past holiday specials have been about as much fun as watching Marley's Ghost drag his chains.

However, Belichick's Army of Zombie Fans cannot get enough of the best coach in the history of football singing his favorite Xmas carols, including "God Rest Ye Merry Steelers," and "Juggled Balls" with Gronk and Cooks.

This year will be even more special than his many past holiday treats.

Tom Brady will be on board for a stocking-stuffer not to be missed. He is expected to reveal that, as he grows younger every day, he has a portrait of Belichick in his attic that grows more sour-looking and ugly with age. You will enjoy it when he presents Belichick with a gift of a "Sock Slider," for oldsters who need help putting on their shoes.

And you thought that was happening every game on the sidelines!

Another highlight of this year's holiday show will be when Gronk puts Coach Belichick on his back and they run around the endzone, doing a turkey trot to celebrate the winning touchdown.

It has been a long hard audition this season to find whether the elves, Amendola and Edelman, will double as Tiny Tim. Giving them a hard run for the job is

Matthew Slater who has been practicing his "God bless us everyone" *ad nauseum.*

Another annual moment of levity shall be when owner Mr. Robert Kraft opens his gifts to discover a lifetime supply of dress shirts with different color collars to go with his only white blouse. Some think Roger Goodell will re-gift Kraft with a draft pick.

Guest appearances by Roger Goodell and Jerry Jones are expected as players will try to dunk them into a big water-tank by tossing footballs at them from a kneeling position.

President Trump will lie about producing the show and tweet that he was going to be extra special guest of the year, but turned them down. He will then fire Tom Brady.

Marshawn Lynch is expected to spoil the big holiday eggnog when he does a Mexican hat-dance with Belichick, and it brings a thunderstorm over Mexico City.

NFL Network, Roku, Apple TV, and Brit Box are clamoring for exclusive rights to show this annual extravaganza of joy and end-zone celebrations.

Don't miss this once-in-a-lifetime, annual tradition (again).

It's Badenov, Oddjob!

First, it was Boris Badenov. Then, it was Oddjob. Now it's even worse: Bill Belichick has gone blackhat.

Rats are now departing the sinking ship of S.S. Philly Eagles.

Not one mouse could deal with the image of the man who made fame in cut-off sweat shirts appearing like the pall-bearer for the underdogs of football.

The Eagle has not landed. It's been grounded.

When Bill Belichick, of hoodie fame, donned a Fedora and black suit when he deplaned the Kraft One Jet, augurs went bonkers.

Magnetic north has shifted. Oddsmakers are scurrying for cover.

Not since the Corleone family flew into Vegas has there been such a fashion statement.

You know the villain always wears the black hat, but the film *noir* world just found its new Robert Mitchum—and he is the man holding all the cards and likely carrying a concealed weapon under his coat.

Frostbite Falls just went into heart seizure. The Super Bowl has just become the Super Bowler. Oddjob worked for Goldfinger and wore a Fedora with a steel-lined brim.

People are prepared to duck if Belichick throws his hat into the Super Bowl ring.

Frostbite Falls, Minnesota, has not seen a Fedora like this since Bullwinkle battled Boris Badenuv on the *Rocky Show.*

Two Bills & Lots of Sense

The Two Bills are sitting at a table longer than the one shared by Citizen Kane and his estranged wife.

ESPN's latest documentary is a look at the remarkable relationship of two NFL coaches who figure prominently in the conversation of greats.

Bill Parcells and Bill Belichick cannot merely be compared as winning NFL coaches. They actually have linked together and bonded in a variety of ways over 40 years.

To put them together at a table in the football Giants locker room and let them watch and listen to clips may actually be a device to give viewers fireworks, contradictions, and hostility. Nothing could be further from the actual event.

You may be surprised what a loud extrovert and a introspective quiet man have in common. They were never friends, but were always respectful colleagues— even at times when tense competition separated them.

What they do have in common is an irascible controlling attitude. It may boil down to the kind of relationship you'd expect between an elder brother and his over-achieving younger sibling. They were rivals, but under the skin shared too much to be anything but blood kin.

Parcells always regretted not being more diplomatic and less inclined to fly off the handle. On the other hand, Belichick admired the way his mentor could deal with the media and see the big picture.

It winds up being a mutual admiration society now that the days of fiery fights across the field have come to an end. They have played golf together and enjoyed dinner to reconcile their former differences after the Jets flare-up when Belichick declined to be drafted into a bad coaching situation, as the heir apparent to Parcells. A Greek chorus of football greats and witnesses to their flare-ups and cool-downs adds to the history lesson.

Owner Robert Kraft slips between them, owing to fancy editing by the director, and notes the complex troubles of managing difficult coaches. It's business, not friendship. It's living with a colleague for years and never socially.

The Two Bills is a fascinating portrait of hard-driven men doing what they love with people they grow to love.

Systemic Problem in NFL

The two foremost social thinkers of the 19[th]century remain powerful symbols of racial injustice: the NFL now claims it did not listen to those uppity black players who believe they are living in an unequal and unjust system of police rioters.

The two biggest symbols of the NFL --Jerry Jones and Bill Belichick—have maintained their deafening silence on the subject of George Floyd and racial brutality.

Their defenders claim that, in private, both are dismayed that their black players are not happy. But, they are not moved much more than Trump on the scale of justice. Oh, yes, they are both MAGA men.

 In the Massachusetts senator debate last night, Joe Kennedy, grandson and great-nephew of Robert and John Kennedy said the Patriots ought to sign Colin Kaepernick. Fat chance: that white snowball in hell belongs to the NFL.

Oh, yes, Robert Kraft is a Trump supporter too.

Defenders of the symbols of NFL victory lappers will never come out and admit their worlds are backward and their views are racist.

It's hard to draw any other conclusion in the face of such rampant ostrich head burying.

There are those rednecks who line the streets holding automatic weapons as a show to intimidate peaceful demonstrators. There are those resemble the Boston

Strangler who put a knee to the neck of the helpless victims but wear police uniforms or NFL neckties.

85% of America think the country is out of control. Among the minority here are Jerry Jones and Bill Belichick: they are always in control, even if your civil rights are thrown out the window.

These are members of the Orange Pips.

Not The Next Patriot QB?

Failing to find a Baker or a Mayfield at the NFL draft, so long, Baker Mayfield, or Baking Maybe, it looks like the Patriots of New England may be in a "heads, you lose/tails, you lose" situation when it comes to Tom's follow-up.

It's beginning to look like a basketball game after the NFL draft, and the Patriots need a sixth man to spell Tom Brady as he reaches into his Social Security years.

To save their 40s old quarterback, the Belichick team may need to sit him halfway through the third quarter of every game, and well into the fourth. Perhaps they merely play him every other game this season.

Or perhaps he sits down when the game is out of hand or in hand. He needs his rest. Keep him hydrated and ready.

In this week's episode of Grabbing Headlines, Tom Brady himself stated how much he appreciates those who kneel during the National Anthem. His owner Robert Kraft said the same words reportedly to other billionaire owners of NFL teams at a meeting.

If any team is going to tackle the Trump approach, it may be the Patriots. If any team can afford to lose fans who have already given up on football because they hate kneelers (except in church apparently).

The NFL has already lost ten or twenty percent of its racist fans. Good riddance.

Are you listening, Colin Kaepernick?

Perhaps in plan two, the Patriots plan to sign Johnny Manziel of Boy Zeal fame. The playboy QB may take a page out of TB12, or AA, depending on how bad he wants to play football.

The Patriots would swirl in controversy for picking up "bad boys" once again and trying to rehab them to win the Super Bowl. It's a scenario usually reserved for Hollywood and the Patriots.

Brady Hates N.E. Weather & Belichick

Once upon a time weather in New England was one of those rare subjects you could talk about safely, no controversy to ensue, no political opinions offered and offended.

Tom Brady, Grifter Emeritus of the Trump Administration, has changed that.

This week in a presser, Brady gave the unsolicited opinion that he would never "be caught dead in the

Northeast again." Nor would he ever be caught in a hoodie or playing for Belichick.

He loves Florida weather. He has not put on a hoodie this year, and he can play outdoors to his heart's content. He did not use the term New England, but Northeast. But we know what he meant. He spent 25 years in hell. Now it's Death in Miami Beach, or Tampa Bay. He calls it Tompa Bay. Yikes.

He plans to build a mansion on Indian Creek Island where there are 30 residents, including Ivanka Trump and Jared Kushner. He will be right at home with his political allies.

Brady gave that number, 25 years, to indicate how long he suffered in the Northeast. Of course, four of those years were in Michigan. Forgive him: he's a general studies major, not too up on things like geography. He can't tell whether Michigan is part of Vermont.

He knows the coldness of Belichick with its mercurial weather has come to an end.

Come to think of it, his math skills seem a little off too. He was in New England 20 years, and 6 Super Bowl titles, 3 flopperoos. So, half his time in cold unpleasant New England weather were his best professional years. And, New England thought he was a natural for cold weather playing.

Of course, Mark Twain once said he counted 70 different kinds of weather in New England in five minute. Tom cannot reach those heights. But, Belichick has sunk into a stupor that indicates he is under a new glacier formation: Cam Newton.

Tompa hated that his son Benjamin played hockey, and that's now over. If you don't play warm weather football, you are skating on thin ice with Tom.

He recently sold his Manhattan condo for $30 million and will never return to New York either. Too cold, especially when it comes to cold cash. The grifter knows his bucks. He took one million from Small Business Admin to infuse his copper-infused TB12 pajama game.

That gave him the down-payment on a hot yacht, and the rest came out of the cold weather profits from selling his overheated condo.

Tom Brady, not exactly a Native Son of New England, though we do feel comfortable in calling him a snow bird.

Belichick is now stuck in the snow drift with his nose up to the cold glass of a losing record.

Tom Wants Out of Belichick's Prison

Now Tom Brady has dumped his 16-year charity work at Best Buddies, where he usually hosts races and football games every year. He is turning the reins over to Jayson Tatum and Julian Edelman.

Do you think Tom's bags are already packed?

If you listen to the experts in Boston sports, apart from us, you have learned this week that Tom Brady is greasing the skids to slide out of town at season's end.

Tom knows which way the wind blows: and it is blowing westward toward the San Andreas fault, where Tom can shake the earth on his own terms. Perhaps he sees Miami as the retirement home of his dreams!

We must agree with the details that Tom Brady is done in Boston, though the bigger picture may be smaller.

It seems that Tom has two reasons to leave: and they are Bill Belichick and Robert Kraft, both of whom have left him stranded without a receiving corps in an annual denuding of first-rate players. Whenever Tom finds someone to his liking, that player is sent packing for reasons usually salary-related.

And Tom remains among the lowest paid superstars at QB position. Taking a hit for the team has grown tiresome for Tom.

It may be that Tom wants to prove, finally, in his golden years, that it is he, not Belichick, who won six Super Bowls. If New England wants a seventh, he may provide it on the way out. The door may slam on someone's ass—but it won't be Tom. Bill Belichick will stay on. Perhaps Josh McDaniel, beloved Babe, will follow out west.

Tom can win two or three more Super Bowls playing for the Raiders in his hometown. Fifty may be the new retirement goal.

Then again, Tommy—and Belichick too—want to show they never needed the other to win the next SB. Unfortunately, they both do need each other—and only will a final separation prove it to them and to the world. Belichick will hold on until his son can become the new King of the Patriots coaching corps.

For fans it will be too late.

In the meantime, Tom snipes at the Boston press—whom he has grown to dislike more than ever—and he and his best friend-trainer, the Svengali of TB12 methodology—have put their Massachusetts homes up for sale in prep for the next season in Oakland.

Yes, you can go home, Tom. And Boston was never home, even after 20 years of suffering through fame and fortune, bad weather and a hundred-fold of receivers.

Taking Belichick Down with Him

All metaphors are imperfect, and nothing could be more imperfect than the notion of Trump at the Alamo. It's the ultimate union of insanity and patriotism.

The fighters who died to the death at the Alamo wanted to have a separate country in Texas. They were the original Republicans.

In movies and TV, you saw John Wayne and Fess Parker play their careers to the hilt of martyrdom on the screen. And, now the disgraced POTUS who instigated sedition and high crimes on a level with Aaron Burr wants to play himself as the end closes in.

He makes it worse for his supporters when he decides to give the Ultimate New England Patriot, Bill Belichick, a gift for his support; the Medal of Freedom as one of his last disgusting acts. It's typical for a man who started his political rise by bashing Mexicans as rapists and drug dealers and ends with the symbol of a wall against Mexico at the bastion where Mexican soldiers killed Davy Crockett and Jim Bowie.

Belichick intends to visit the White House as the Congress votes a second impeachment of Trump. Who is the mad man here? We count Belichick among the NFL cheaters with Spygates 1 & 2 and Trump with Impeachment 1 & 2.

And, now, the Patriots should fire Belichick, sacrifice to the cause of a *coup d'etat,* the supporter of Trump and coach of historical arrogance and now hostage to his own hubris.

Losing the season, losing Tom Brady, and losing his mind, Bill Belichick now will regain infamy by going to the White House and accepting honor from a man who has made honor a badge to kill legislators at the U.S. Capitol, and claim he was a victim of voters.

If the owners of the Patriots do not fire Bill Belichick for this egregious act, then we have the demise of a franchise, self-perpetuated by the Kraft family (Trumpists too and big lonely New England supporters of the American Hitler) in the most of antithetical states standing against Trump: New England went overwhelmingly for anybody but Trump.

We are watching the spectacle of the last gasp of a political movement and the gasping greed of a sports dynasty. America never had it so wrong and may be sinking into its own miasma of Nazism, white supremacy, and stupidity.

Belichick Declines Trump's Medal

We may never know how much angst and conflict New England Patriot coach Bill Belichick suffered in coming to his decision to turn down the Medal of Freedom. A few have pointed out that he did not actually turn it down, but may have faced forces in the sports world that required him to say, "no."

The honor came from a political ally whom he supported once upon a time. Today is not a time to be nostalgic for past loyalty when present conditions may be dubious.

It is a prestigious award, and under normal circumstance, it would be the culmination of honor in a life. Yet, after sedition broke out in the Capitol and some died as a result, the 6-time winner of the Super

Bowl knew that honor and flattery must never cover up a cynical attempt to be used by a friend for political reasons.

Yes, it's true that Belichick would look like a man who condoned a set of values that might reverberate in negative ways among players and fans.

Though he always disdains media, the New England fixture cannot lose sight of the prize: his eye is on the sparrow, not the fake glory that comes from accepting a tarnished award.

It may be that another president will give him this honor. We hope so. Representing the concept of American victory in sports may not be what some consider a worthy reason. Perhaps not, but Trump has given this award to plenty of people who never deserved it.

Some have accepted the award under dubious clouds, like Rep. Jim Jordan, a water-boy, not a coach whose career and attitude belie the Medal of Freedom. Others could return the honor, like Boston Celtic legend Bob Cousy, but he hasn't. Obama gave Bill Russell the Medal of Freedom for his work on Civil Rights.

Bill's work on players' rights has been somewhat limited.

"Belicheat!" Exclaimed Don Shula

Is it possible there is no photo of Bill Belichick and Don Shula ever standing together? They hated each other enough that you can find no eulogy from Belichick to the winningest coach in NFL history when he died in 2020.

In 2015 Shula called Belichick by the untoward nickname of "Belicheat." When he died, Belichick issued a terse statement of facts: Shula and his father knew each other. End of story.

Or is it? Shula coached for 33 years, and Belichick has now reached 25 seasons. But, at age 69, the Patriots head coach will be approaching 80 if he lasts that long.

It's possible, of course, as Joe Biden is taking over as President of the United States at that age.

Also, Bill will need to have ten winning seasons to reach a threshold above and beyond Shula. Is that possible if he continues to work with stiff QBs like Cam Newton who gave him his first losing season in 20 years?

The fewer winning seasons, more years will be required to overcome Shula. The Patriot coach has six Super Bowl victories that far outweighs anyone else, but Shula has that undefeated season that weighs heavily on Belichick.

Time is not always kind or sympathetic to movie villains, or even sports villains. Belicheat may be looking at come-uppance.